CARPATHIA

Also by Cecilia Woloch

Sacrifice (1997)
Tsigan: The Gypsy Poem (2002)
Late (2003)
Narcissus (2008)

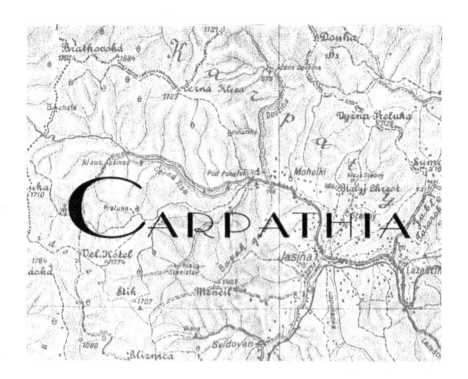

Poems by

CECILIA WOLOCH

AMERICAN POETS CONTINUUM SERIES, NO. 117

BOA Editions, Ltd. ✴. Rochester, NY ✴. 2009

09 10 11 12 7 6 5 4 3 2

For information about permission to reuse any material from this book please contact
The Permissions Company at www.permissionscompany.com or e-mail permdude@
eclipse.net.

Publications by BOA Editions, Ltd.—a not-for-profit corporation under section 501 (c) (3)
of the United States Internal Revenue Code—are made possible with funds from a variety
of sources, including public funds from the New York State Council on the Arts, a state
agency; the Literature Program of the National Endowment for the Arts; the County of
Monroe, NY; the Lannan Foundation for support of the Lannan Translations Selection
Series; the Sonia Raiziss Giop Charitable Foundation; the Mary S. Mulligan Charitable
Trust; the Rochester Area Community Foundation; the Arts & Cultural Council for
Greater Rochester; the Steeple-Jack Fund; the Ames-Amzalak Memorial Trust in memory
of Henry Ames, Semon Amzalak and Dan Amzalak; and contributions from many indi-
viduals nationwide. See Colophon on page 84 for special individual acknowledgments.

Cover Design: Sandy Knight
Cover Art: Jonde Northcutt
Interior Design and Composition: Richard Foerster

BOA Logo: Mirko

Library of Congress Cataloging-in-Publication Data

Woloch, Cecilia, 1956–
Carpathia : poems / Cecilia Woloch. — 1st ed.
     p. cm.
ISBN 978-1-934414-26-2 (alk. paper)
I. Title.
PS3573.O5677C37 2009
811'.54—dc22
                                2009020529

BOA Editions, Ltd.

NATIONAL
ENDOWMENT
FOR THE ARTS
A great nation
deserves great art.

State of the Arts

NYSCA

A. Poulin, Jr., Founder (1938-1996)
250 North Goodman Street, Suite 306
Rochester, NY 14607
www.boaeditions.org

Contents

III

for Lynn Chanté Whitley-Head
sister-friend
2/13/63–10/15/06

We all dwell in one country, O stranger, the world.
                                        —Meleager

I

Postcard with Sarah, to Sarah, from a Bridge in Paris— Which?

It's late and we've stopped to lean against the rail of the Pont Marie. Or the Pont Louis-Philippe. Or some other bridge—which bridge? It's cloudy; the moon is veiled. Or it's clear, but we can't see the Tour Eiffel. Below us, on the quai, there's a kind of party going on. Someone's about to fall into the river, or about to plunge, or he's being pushed. Or, no, it was only a game, after all. See?—they're laughing. A joke among friends. My friend who leans beside me is saying she wants another child. Now she's sure of it. A boy. Or another girl like the girl she has. Or different. More like the father. Or darker, this time, like herself. What does it matter? Either one. Either one of us could be the other, sometimes. In shadow, like this. She sighs. We both stare down at the glittering river knowing we'll find no answers there. We've agreed there's no right or wrong, no answers at all when it comes to love. And there are so many we might have loved, might yet love, or love again. Her husband, she says, *still recovering from the shock* of her being his wife. *I'm not winking, it's just my eye.* And we're falling down laughing. We're standing here. *So beautiful,* one of us says. Or the other thinks. The river, the wind. It's cold and our coats are thin. It's spring and the blossoms the trees breathe scatter like petals of snow at our feet. It's the middle of our lives, and night, and we walk toward everything.

Didn't I stand there once?
Didn't I choose to go back?
—Patricia Hooper, "Narcissus"

Anniversary

Didn't I stand there once,
white-knuckled, gripping the just-lit taper,
swearing I'd never go back?
And hadn't you kissed the rain from my mouth?
And weren't we gentle and awed and afraid,
knowing we'd stepped from the room of desire
into the further room of love?
And wasn't it sacred, the sweetness
we licked from each other's hands?
And were we not lovely, then, were we not
as lovely as thunder, and damp grass, and flame?

Shine

In such dark times, we all need to shine—
each to each, with what light we have,
as dusk like a smoky curtain falls
from east to west across the world
and the world grows dim with news of war
and the headlines blacken our fingertips
and the wicks of candles burnt to char—
among these monuments and shadows,
friends, let us suffer our radiance.

In this city in which I once loved my beloved
in hunger, the brasseries shine
and the neon of St. Michel casts a glow like dawn
on the ancient walls
and the wine in our glasses, ruby and bright,
and the teeth of the waiter when he smiles
and our voices like coins in our throats
and our laughter, silver as ever, and all our tears,
useless and beautiful, shine.

And the Seine gleams darkly past,
dragging its net of drowning stars
and the half-moon, tarnished gold, slides
through the ragged map of clouds
and somewhere the sky being torn
into sheets of flame and shrieking shines.

And the paving stones shine beneath
the clatter of our heels in the courtyard's hush
and the window of one room, blue,
glows in the loneliness of its night
and the flickering light of the TV screen
buzzes and shines with its shining lies

and our reflections thrown back from the glass—
our ghosts in the gilt-framed mirrors shine.

And our prayers, which are nothing, shine
and the bones of the dead in the earth's black loam
and the flowers on graves with their dumb, sweet tongues
and my wedding band, small and gold, still whole
and the whole bloody planet, glimpsed
through the eye of what god may yet
squint through the stars at us, shines.

Postcard to Ilya Kaminsky from a Dream at the Edge of the Sea

I was leaving a country of rain for a country of apples. I hadn't much time. I told my beloved to wear his bathrobe, his cowboy boots, a black patch like a pirate might wear over his sharpest eye. My own bags were full of salt, which made them shifty, hard to lift. Houses had fallen, face first, into the mud at the edge of the sea. *Hurry*, I thought, and my hands were like birds. They could hold nothing. A feathery breeze. Then a white tree blossomed over the bed, all white blossoms, a painted tree. *"Oh,"* I said, or my love said to me. We want to be human, always, again, so we knelt like children at prayer while our lost mothers hushed us. A halo of bees. I was dreaming as hard as I could dream. It was fast—how the apples fattened and fell. The country that rose up to meet me was steep as a mirror; the gold hook gleamed.

What Is This?

—*after "Have Broken Up," by Melanie Braverman*

It's a pillow for the invisible, a pillow for shadows, a pillow for ghosts.
It's a pillow against which the heads of the dead are lain to awaken them.
The edges have been stitched by hand by angels using thorns.
See this whiteness broken only by itself? It isn't sky.
It isn't even what you thought asleep you were, those clouds you dreamt.
A page on which the words *Je t'embrasse* appear, then fade.
The luminous surface startles like water across which no such wind
    has swept.

Greed

I was his, everything was his—

even my sleep belonged to him.
Even my rising, almost weightless
—bride of everything—was his.

Sun tossed like coins across the bed,
and the glittering of birdsong, breeze
the cool blue of his eyes. Even the mirror

where a woman, shining, turned
to kiss be kissed. Even the shallow, silvered glass
in which I dressed, undressed, was his.

And then I thought to speak again.
And then I dared, made flesh, to want
my own two hands, my blood luck back.

And he grew ravenous, enraged,
and all the spilt world poured
into the cup from which he drank.

Postcard to Lisa, with Lisa, from Metro Line 1

No one had seen him before he fell, but we saw the man fall. To his knees in the aisle of the train. Then face down, as if in prayer, forehead pressed to the filthy floor. Someone gasped. Someone called out, *Monsieur! Monsieur?* Someone tried to lift him up, but he lurched and fell back the other way. Backwards, hitting the back of his head. That's when we saw the gash in his scalp. Was it a fresh wound or a scar? There was no blood. He did not seem drunk. A neatly-dressed, dark-skinned man, though the cuffs of his trousers were frayed. Someone tumbled him into a seat and he sat there and would not or could not speak. I reached over and pulled the alarm. The doors slid open but no one came. I leapt from the car and ran down the quai and rapped at the glass conductor's cage. The conductor was standing inside, in darkness, watching the scene on a little screen. I could not think of what to say in French. *Un homme. Il est tombé.* And then he was standing over the dazed man, naming the stations of the metro, asking where the man wanted to go. But the man wouldn't talk; his eyes stayed closed. A clochard stepped into the car, drunk and smelling of vomit and piss. He started yelling—trying to help? The other passengers cleared a path. Some had just sat there all along. A young girl clipping her fingernails furiously, clippings falling into her lap. The dazed man was taken out onto the quai. Still not speaking. The train pulled away. The clochard had stayed on board, now he was filling the car with his stench. Someone leaned over my seat and whispered (in English), *This doesn't happen here that much.*

Mistake

Near the end, he thought he saw death
near the door where his dark robe hung.
But it was only his robe in the dark.
It was only the door. It was only his death
come for him, and near.

Sleep, I begged him, *Sleep*.
And he lifted one hand into the air—
pale hand, almost blue in that dark.
As if waving hello or goodbye, or trying
to touch his own life as it passed.

Last Fever

The last I knew of my father's body alive
was the fever that wouldn't break.
I bent with my mother over the bed,
pressing cool rags to his forehead, his chest,
turning the body—what was left of the body—
first this way, then that, to be touched.
His temperature fell, then rose again.
His flesh gave off heat as if something burned in him
that could only be quenched by death.
Still, we worked until 4 A.M.,
dipping our rags in the basin, our hands
moving over the body's ruined landscape like flags
in some kind of surrender, surrendering him.

Brasov, 1989

—on a photograph by David Turnley

The women are waiting in line to confess—
standing or slumping or leaning on canes
or half-crouched, backs pressed to the wall
of a wooden church in Brasov, Romania.
It's the Year of Our Lord, 1989; six months before
all hell will break loose, and the brute
who's starved them—a nation of starvelings—
will be shot, point-blank, in the head.

The women's faces are calm, or grim
—one might wonder, *Where are the men?*—
but the light is golden, warm, diffuse,
as if all sins, once confessed, or desires
(who has butter today? has meat? an egg?)
could be left at the feet of a wooden saint
with a whisper, a kiss, a prayer for forgiveness:
Because we've been broken. Because we've obeyed.

Postcard Beginning with a Quote from Mark C., Avenue de l'Opéra

I was *a ripe plum* that summer, he said, *so thin-skinned and full, so ready to fall.* How to un-want what the body has wanted, explain how the flesh in its wisdom was wrong? If we say: *the stars.* If we say: *some ghost in the mind; some blue chemical rushing the blood.* If we say: *some demon or god—?* We were never as beautiful as we thought. The pictures prove nothing and memory fails. Tonight on the metro a woman lay her head on the chest of a man and wept. He seemed to be trying to comfort her. She seemed to be struggling not to sob. I walked up from the station into the street, stood in the square that faces L'Opéra: gilded domes against rose-tinged sky. The world seemed so glamorous, didn't it, once? And that was my fault, how I wished and fell. In my best moments, looking back, this is what I tell myself: I've wanted only to sleep and dream and wake in some country my heart could call home. What I want to tell you now is to let go of everything. I have. Let go the wind that lifts the hair from the nape of my neck, this faded scarf. Let go the rage you felt, or desire, when you watched me walk away from you. I never belonged in a world but this world. It rained. Every room was a borrowed room.

House

In the house of be-quiet-and-sleep
In the house of no apples and sharpened knives
In the house where your father would not come to live
    if your mother died
    or your mother, your father
In the house of fat bees falling into the wine
    swatted mid-swoon
    in their lust for flowers
In the house of cut flowers, cut green
    at their throats and stripped
    of their petals, breath by breath
In the house like a narrow box tilted askew
    in which we were shaken like broken toys
In the house of the doll of our lord the unkind
In the house of shut-up-and-lock-the-doors
    and only one door to the world, one to sky

Lethe

I remember the day you started
hating yourself again. Almost the hour.
That death mask come over
your face. More skull than flesh.
The harsh light. Wind.
How you looked on that cliff
overlooking the city. How you refused
to turn and look. Your eyes
two holes for sky. Your mouth
a grim line. Thin. How we walked
hand-in-hand along the ruined river—
river of shadows. How I wept.
How you plucked from the grass
a single flower by its throat
to shut me up. You called it
the black dog, your bitterness,
laughed. We wandered past dusk,
until we were lost, until you saw
some place to drink and went in.
I watched you lifting the glass to your lips
again and again. Of thirst. Of spite.
Hating yourself, hating me. Hating
that city, its wind and its dogs
and its filthy river. Your life.

Postcard from Akhmatova's Bed

March threw its knives against the door. Lucky for me, that room had a bolt
and chain, a window with green in its eye. I slept with a book of poems
for a pillow—the collected works of Anna Akhmatova, who'd lived
through siege and war—and I listened and tried not to listen for your
furious tread on the stairs. We were all dead roses, then, and you flung
my lingerie down the hall. Little clicks of the snaps and hooks. Little
gasps of silk as silk slid down the walls. I dreamt one night that I rescued
Akhmatova; took her away from the gray block of flats in that city where
she'd grown old, and back to her Russian dacha to die. A small wooden
house in a forest of birch, trees slender as brides; the house painted red.
Then she was gone, but she'd left me the key to the dacha, her wooden
bed shaped like a boat. I led you there and lay down; I begged you to lie
down, but you refused. Spring or no spring, you wouldn't budge; bed of
the famous poet or not. It was March then, all thorn and bud. It was the
end of a terrible winter and, when I awoke, I had sky in my mouth.

Lucifer, Full of Light

And if I should pick out the good in you—
each shard of broken light, like glass
from the wreck of such beauty, and look at that—

or one golden afternoon when you hovered above me
in rapture, oh half god—

how would I bear to lift my hands,
how would I bear to close my eyes
and let you fall, and love be damned?

Salt

What you wanted from salt was salt.
What you wanted from each of the bones of my hand was touch like a
    river, smoke.
What you wanted from smoke was the holy body ghostly to the mind.
What you wanted from the body was a body that would not die.
What you wanted from fire was heat and light, but also char, the flare
    of sparks.
What you wanted I had to give but to make it small enough to crush.
What you wanted to crush was the quick hand, river, birds, the field in
    flames.
And then what you wanted was salt, a woman weeping at your back,
but you could not turn to look.

Postcard to X from Warsaw, Ulica Piękna ("Pretty Street")

The old woman selling flowers next to the archway at ulica Piękna was wearing orange lipstick today. Shiny orange lipstick, and a smile; her black kerchief knotted under her chin. She was smoking a cigarette, all her tulips arranged in plastic tubs at her feet—gaudily purple and yellow and red. I could tell she felt quite the coquette, and it made her mouth look lovely, in fact. That slick of peach on her lips as she sat with her back to the flat gray wall. The building behind her a relic, too. My friend says the communists built these apartments *to show the workers how they might live.* Though only the highest officials—most brutal, most damned—were given such balconies, of course. Everyone else in the dreary blocks built on the ash of the murdered, the crushed, stinking forever of cabbage and piss. But today there was rain, here in Warsaw, then sun. The wind had shifted, then shifted again. The clouds moved like swans across the sky. And the old woman—I passed her twice—made a few zlotys on flowers, I'd guess. She sat there for hours on Pretty Street, her mouth like a pearl in her wrinkled face. And you—you know who you are; you tried to be human once but you failed—could not have touched this woman. Ever. She, with her tulips. Not bitter. Nor I.

Watching Him Die

It was horrible
but it wasn't all horrible.

There were days he had to be bathed and changed like a child—
the stink of ammonia, the glimpse
of loose flesh on bony limbs
(the mirror covered to keep him calm);
the sores on his back
that would not heal.

There were evenings he staggered down the hallway,
touching the walls,
thinking the house was on fire;
nights he raged, *Just let me out*,
turned over furniture, spit pills.

And so there were nights
(too many nights)
we had to tie him into bed
and he thrashed and he wept
and my mother tried to sleep beside him
or I slept beside his bed on the floor.

But there were also moments of grace—
when he sang in Ukrainian, *little bird*;
when he kissed the hand that brought food to his lips,
kissed the food,
kissed a sugar donut, once.

The stuttered *Thank you*
when I cut the meat on his plate.
The heavy hand on the top of my head—
the whole weight of fatherhood in that touch.

And then there was death,
which did not come gently,
but gently enough.
Enough of the flung chairs and sirens wailing,
enough of the weeping and stuttering.
Enough of the mind erasing itself
until there was nothing of language left,
nothing of how to breathe again.

And then in that room the smell of flowers,
though there were no flowers there.

Ground

Someone we loved is under this ground so we all come back and call it
    home.

So what if the grave is a few miles away—down a twisting road
where the redbud blooms, where a barbed wire fence
between the nearest house and the high grass turns to rust?

Wherever I am, wherever I walk, my feet touch the earth and my
    heart says *bone.*

Midnight: I sweep through the sleeping rooms, more guest than
    daughter now.
One of my brothers sighs through the wall, snoring the way our father
    snored.

Oh body, old screen door.

Outside, the crickets are singing the grass alive; a train passes. Where
    are we now?

If this is Kentucky, my father said once, squinting up through the clouds,
that must be the moon.

And this is the place my father chose to be buried in, so I must be home.
So I must walk barefoot across the lawn in a pair of pajamas he left
    when he died—because he took nothing—and call to him.

Ghost Hunger

Sometimes when I wipe the bowl with my bread
when I scramble one egg, two eggs, with milk

when I stir the kasha until it's thick
when I sit at the table and bow my head

I think of how my father ate
how he bowed his head—though he didn't pray

at least not in the usual way of grace
but always that posture over his plate

of supplication, gratitude—
the hungry shoulders of the boy

who'd stuffed his mouth with pulled grass once
who never got over that there was enough

Sometimes I wipe the bowl with my bread
Sometimes I feed his ghost this prayer

Postcard to Myself from the Lower Carpathians, Spring

I slept in a room filled with white moths. In a wooden house in the lower Carpathians—*Beskid Niski*—each silvery night. I made my bed in the room's far corner, white moths settling like quiet petals on every surface as evening fell. They folded their wings and clung to the walls without a quiver as I undressed. I knew, as soon as I switched off the lamp, that the air would go pale with their fluttering. I knew, in my sleep, one might light on my arm, on my cheek, in my hair, without waking me. In this room, also, the seeds of wildflowers gleaned from the meadows were spread out to dry. What I learned about gentleness then. What I learned to be gently less wary of. I want not to forget those nights in the lower Carpathians, deep spring, sleeping alone: the white moths swirling as I dreamt; the meadows baring themselves to the moon.

II

Why I Believed, as a Child, That People Had Sex in Bathrooms

Because they loved one another, I guessed.
Because they had seven kids and there wasn't
a door in that house that was ever locked—
except for the bathroom door, that door
with the devil's face, two horns like flame
flaring up in the grain of the wood
(or did we only imagine that shape?)
which meant the devil could watch you pee,
the devil could see you naked.
Because that's where people took off their clothes
and you had to undress for sex, I'd heard,
whatever sex was—lots of kissing and other stuff
I wasn't sure I wanted to know.
Because at night, when I was scared, I just
climbed into my parents' bed. Sometimes
other kids were there, too, and we slept
in a tangle of sheets and bodies, breath;
a full ashtray on the nightstand; our father's
work clothes hung over a chair; our mother's
damp cotton nightgown twisted around her legs.
Because when I heard babies were made from sex
and sex was something that happened in bed,
I thought: *No, the babies are already there*
in the bed. And more babies came.

Because the only door that was ever locked
was the bathroom door—those two inside
in the steam of his bath, her hairspray's mist,
because sometimes I knocked and was let in.
And my father lay in the tub, his whole dark body
underwater, like some beautiful statue I'd seen.
And my mother stood at the mirror, fixing her hair,
or she'd put down the lid of the toilet

and perched there, talking to him.
Because maybe this was their refuge from us—
though they never tried to keep us away.
Because my mother told me once
that every time they came home from the hospital
with a brand new baby, they laughed
and fell in love all over again
and couldn't wait to start making more.
Should this have confused me? It did not.
Because I saw how he kissed the back of her neck
and pulled her, giggling, into his lap;
how she tucked her chin and looked up at him
through her eyelashes, smiling, sly.
So I reasoned whatever sex they had, they had
in the bathroom—those steamy hours
when we heard them singing to one another
then whispering, and the door stayed locked.

Because I can still picture them, languid, there,
and beautiful and young—though I had no idea
how young they were—my mother
soaping my father's back; her dark hair
slipping out of its pins...
Because what was sex, after that? I didn't know
he would ever die, this god in a body, strong as god,
or that she would one day hang her head
over the bathroom sink to weep. I was a child,
only one of their children. Love was clean.
Babies came from singing. The devil was wood
and had no eyes.

to sing love
Love must first shatter us

—H.D., "Eros"

Postcard to Ben, with Ben, from Paris, Kentucky

This is the green we grew up in—the humid blue of the blur of our adolescence; the weedy heat. These are the roads we drove *into the country* with whoever had sweet, cheap wine. The song of gnat and firefly and nightingale and frog. This is the sky of watery silk under which we wrecked our hearts, cried out. Wild onion in the high grass, and magnolia—cloud of blossoms—where we lay some nights till dawn beside *the one, the one, the only one,* and then another love. This is the place I chose exile from, sharp-hearted, sure of some brighter world. And still, how it takes me back. How the dark trees make a leafy arch above us as we pass. How you grip the wheel and laugh, don't say, *Remember.* Don't say anything.

Fireflies

And these are my vices:
impatience, bad temper, wine,
the more than occasional cigarette,
an almost unquenchable thirst to be kissed,
a hunger that isn't hunger
but something like fear, a staunching of dread
and a taste for bitter gossip
of those who've wronged me—for bitterness—
and flirting with strangers and saying *sweetheart*
to children whose names I don't even know
and driving too fast and not being Buddhist
enough to let insects live in my house
or those cute little toylike mice
whose soft gray bodies in sticky traps
I carry, lifeless, out to the trash
and that I sometimes prefer the company of a book
to a human being, and humming
and living inside my head
and how as a girl I trailed a slow-hipped aunt
at twilight across the lawn
and learned to catch fireflies in my hands,
to smear their sticky, still-pulsing flickering
onto my fingers and earlobes like jewels.

Faith

I once believed in ridiculous things: the ghosts of swans; the wings of death; that fire leapt from the tip of the match, a living thing; in magic; luck. Was I wrong to slip sugar under my pillow at night, wrong to kiss photographs? I believed in the kind of god who granted wishes. Any god. In trees with their terrible faces of bark. Even on my knees, I believed what I'd lost would be given back. Whole rosaries of grief; the painted saints breathing when I breathed. What makes a child who's scratched her own hands until they're raw have faith like that? Light in the gravel she skidded across; light in her blood and the jewel of the scab. When I look back, I see how foolish it was to try to shape those clouds. I lay in the grass. Birds fell into sky. The dead were fruitful; they multiplied.

Who Reminds Me of You, When You Could Still Walk,
—Just Barely

Any old man,
back to me, slightly stooped,
walking along beside the road,
half-turning but not
quite turning around
to catch me
watching him,
because he is vanishing,
already, already
seems to himself
like a ghost
and could be you,
those wasting years
when the world let go
of you, let go—
and the numb sun shone
like a halo, too bright
through all the sparse
white hairs of your head.

Seven Years After Your Death,

I'm still waiting for you to appear
in the feathery clouds, my heaven-gone father,
if there's a heaven. It's rush hour here.

Across the street, the leafy campus, calm and grave
in late autumn sun. But the traffic's brisk—
a bright stream flashing; too swift to risk—so I wait;

warm cup of milky tea clutched in one hand,
folders and textbooks tucked under my arm,
the light unchanging—*oh world without end*—

and I'm thinking I'll stand here forever, stuck,
when a friend drives past, waving, calling my name,
and I can't wave back so I raise my cup

and then some old man in a truck waves, too
—just an old man in a battered red pickup—
but I laugh, raise my cup to him, thinking of you

and you touch my cheek, then, or seem to—a breeze
that sighs, *What a mess you've made of your life*
—married twice, twice-divorced—then your voice

says, *You'll love again, honey, there's time.*
And the bright stream parts, so I make a run for it,
cross unharmed to the other side.

Girl in a Truck, Kentucky Highway 245

It all comes back to me, almost near enough to touch—this shimmering: redbud blooming beside the road; sunlight shattering through the leaves. And a blue haze draped like a gauzy veil across the distance I'm driving toward. Late afternoon, still early spring. How, as a girl, in cut-off jeans and a skimpy string-bikini top, I lay in the back of a pickup truck, the better to bronze my young, bare flesh. How I wanted to scorch myself, then; how I wanted to burn my beauty onto the very eye of love.

How lovely, the way we wreck ourselves on the world; how we shine in it, too.

How I almost wave, now, at the girl standing up in the bed of the truck in the yard I pass. I remember myself at that age, remember the longing, almost like rage, to touch and be touched, and my innocence. I've slipped a bleeding heart, tiny bud, into the cup of my lacy bra: crushed petals pressed against my breast. I've come back to save what can still be saved of the girl who believed—who goes on believing, shattered and shimmering, driving too fast—that the beloved, oh beloved, all bright tenderness, will come.

My Old True Love

My campesino,
barefoot
in the kitchen,
3 A.M.,
jeans rolled to your calves.
My sling-shot lover,
dog-shit mogul,
king of beans
and garlic, wine.
My melancholy whistler,
sleek delinquent,
darker twin.
My outlaw of the roses
through the fence.
My unplucked plum.
My *hey-young-lady* of a man.
My dear,
my love,
my shamed heart shamed.
My dirt-poor prince
among the sparrows
and the power lines,
my friend.

Known

You've cut your hair, I said, and, *Yes*, you smiled
and let me put my hand to the nape of your neck.

There is cruelty in all of us, too, but in some
it has lain down awhile to be soothed.

To be soothed, once, I asked you to hold me
and all night you lay with your arms outstretched.

And when we had woken enough to be calm,
the kiss of forgiveness still warm in our mouths,

it was a new year. Bare trees. All our lives.

Postcard with Andrew, to Andrew, from I-75 on New Year's Day

That afternoon we were driving south through the mountains of Georgia and talked all the way. Winter light shining like grief in your hair, black as the wing of a crow, and like joy. The old year dying around us then; the weather all bright wind, wild and clear. We stopped at a store by the side of the road and got out to kiss in the parking lot. *Just like old times*, I thought, and remembered those years we were tortured and young, meeting like thieves in our guilty coats because we believed in the lawful heart. And I thought, then I said out loud, *We should have just run away.* We might have escaped, then, those other doomed loves. Though maybe those other doomed loves were our fate. Well, now this was our fate: the little black truck, the long conversation taken back up. And that kiss, which was *yes* on your lips—because I'd been talking to you all along. All those nights I'd wept and called your name, driving alone, having nowhere to go. And *yes*, you said, you'd heard. So we got back in the truck like two fugitives, Dark Heart, back on that sky of a road.

Wish

We clean the bones of the little birds we eat
with our teeth, then we let them dry.
Later, we split each wish at the crux—
Many dollars for both of us.

But love, we are vagabonds still,
our sleep full of bells and kisses, wind.
We have never touched one another enough.
We have never completely eaten our fill.

If I covered your body in lilacs now,
pale purple flowers against your dark skin,
would you not shake my breath from your hair
when you stood, would you wish

that the small birds who fed us had lived?

Blazon

—after Breton

My love with his hair of nightingales
With his chest of pigeon flutter, of gray doves preening themselves at
    dawn
With his shoulders of tender balconies half in shadow, half in sun
My love with his long-boned thighs the map of Paris of my tongue
With his ink-stained tongue, his tongue the tip
of a steeple plunged into milky sky
My love with his wishing teeth
With his fingers of nervous whispering, his fingers of a boy
whose toys were cheap and broken easily
My love with his silent thumbs
With his eyes of a window smudged of a train that passes in the night
With his nape of an empty rain coat
hung by the collar, sweetly bowed
My love with his laughter of an empty stairwell, rain all afternoon
With his mouth the deepest flower to which
I have ever put my mouth

Be Always Late

—after Baudelaire

One should always be late. One should always be running/half-running in high-heeled boots through the streets with the church bells ringing the hour one should have already arrived. And be still en route, still a bridge away, still a sliver of silvery river to go. One should have clouds at one's shoulders like breath, panting clouds and a gasp of wind at the nape of the neck to keep one cool. The heart should be clicking against the ribs: *I'm late, I'm late, I'm late.* One should be turning just then past the church, past evening beginning in every cafe, past the poor little park with its late little flowers, disheveled little flames. Because somewhere someone waits. Because somewhere one has already arrived and will never rush past this again. One's self with one's coat like a black sky flung; one's own shadow flaring out behind. And the sound of those bells in one's hair, in one's bones. Now and ever. Not never: late.

Kind Weather

If I have to fall let me fall
with eyes closed, arms spread wide

as if falling naked from Paradise,
or, at least, slip out of this dress—

worn too tight at the hips for years,
worn too thin to be worn again.

Or let it be Paris, the burnished clouds
moving bright-godless across the sky

and love in its delicate, wild blue shoes
tripping all over itself, and rain

as it was on earth when we first began
forever and ever to kiss, amen.

Postcard to Carine from the Past

We were foolish as fool's gold once. We were tinsel and brass. We were such cheap dates. You in your studio in the Village, making the doorman's eyes spin in his head. Me in L.A., which did not love me better or less, with a bed like a parachute. One lover went out for vodka and never returned. One lover scrawled his farewell note on the walls before he left. Whose was whose? Too many to count, and too ridiculous, now, to remember. You had a smile that set trashcans on fire. I had a laugh that scared crows from the trees. No wonder no one stayed for breakfast and so many staggered up from their knees. If I'd known you then, I'd have shaken your bony shoulders, kissed you once, hard, on the mouth. You'd have insisted I eat, anyway. We'd have been young together once, my sister, and none the wiser now.

Pantoum: le Jardin d'Isabelle

The love of my lover for his wife:
his name being stone, the word for stone,
and her name like a flower, *Isabelle*—
who has thrown herself into the garden this summer, made it a paradise.

His name is the stone I polished in my mouth all winter long:
Pierre, as in *Peter*, who stands at the gate,
who welcomes me into the garden this summer she's made a paradise.
And I come bearing the little sin of sweet alyssum, love them both—

Pierre (she calls *Peter*) who stands at the gate,
and Isabelle, coming toward me now, knee-deep in the shimmering grass.
I have brought them the little sin of sweet alyssum, love them both—
and beloved, welcomed, slip into the shade between them, kissed

by the child who's come rushing toward me, waist-deep in the
    shimmering grass
and, lifted into my arms, names me *tante* of weeds and wind
and beloved, laughing, slips into the shade between us, blessed—
the love of this man for this woman and this woman for this child.

And lifting out of my arms the crushed bouquet of weeds and wind
and calling it *luck* the glass I shatter in the offering of wine,
this man who loves this woman who loves this woman who loves this
    child
offers me a place at love's long table. Not cast out,

and calling it *luck*—the glass I shatter in the offering of wine
and the love of my lover for his wife
and my place among them, here, at love's long table, not cast out—
I name every flower, *Isabelle*.

Postcard to Some Beloved, from the Rue des Guillemites

A little sugar falls from the sky and I don't even care tonight that you're gone. Wherever you are or will ever be. It's not some fairy tale, this life, but a few coins are tossed, a few beloveds get onto their knees, there's some weather, at last. If I went down to the street in my blue robe, now, in the cold, in the snow, I could taste the darkness with my eyes and my fingers and mouth. I would not disturb anyone, at this hour. And no one disturbs me—not the old women, faces like parchment under the hoods of their long fur coats; not the men in uniform, flashing along; not the scurrying rats; not the sad, small dogs. Not even the sky is my enemy here, in this city in which I've laid myself down like a page to be written upon. If you tell this story, say there was sweetness and wind; that what fell fell like handfuls of stars—no, like handfuls of sugar. Whose hands? Anyone's.

Whose Hunger

Whose/hunger is a dress for my song
—Brigit Pegeen Kelly

Whose one white note is feast enough
for all the throats of dusk

Whose name is light inside my mouth
a humming light (I will not tell)

Whose story has a child in it
of jade, a child of gold

Whose sorrow can't be kissed away
Who made a sparrow of my heart

Whose brightest ghost my brightest ghost
uncleaves from, cleaves unto

Who stands within the mirror
and the mirror turns to rain

Postcard to Sarah, in the Carpathians, from Paris, the Rue Vieille du Temple

It's twilight and, Sarah, I'm teetering in the woozy blue of it all. Walking: *he loves me; he loves me not.* I could fall to my knees at the river's splendor or button my coat and just cross the bridge. I could do both if my heart were bigger: *love him; love him not.*

A woman lands her bicycle in the midst of the pigeons' ascent. This happens all at once. She glides down the sidewalk, no longer astride, one foot on the pedal, one grazing the ground, as if she's been flying, and just at that moment, the whole flock of birds rises up. The thrumming of wings like a storm in reverse. Like wind and rain flying back toward sky. Which is how, lately, the weather has been.

And you, in your weathered house, in this transparent weather come over us both, writing—even before you've had coffee or woken your daughter—*I understand.* Two things can happen at once: landing; ascent. Let us love in reverse. Let us with wind on the tips of our tongues live those beginnings again and again. How he walked you through dusk to the one bright room. How, in late afternoon, in pink shoes, I led him up three flights of sunlit stairs, then fell—yes, *like roses*—at his feet.

How the birds move in chorus, somehow, as if at a signal. Then how far apart.

Au Revoir, Paris

Loveliest of what we leave behind are the waiters
Flirtatious and quick, sliding in slick-soled shoes
From table to tiny table, winking and clinking the silver
And singing us sweet, sweet *Mademoiselles*

And loveliest after those the Mademoiselles with their sleep-strewn hair
With their careless scarves at their delicate throats
With their serious books on their laps as the metro glides toward St.
    Michel

And also *les vieilles hommes* who grunt and sigh as we Pardon past
And the old *mesdames* with their little dogs
Trotting along beside their ankles of terrible woe but no regret

And lovely the dog shit we dodge on the sidewalks, piles of it
Gleaming and green with flies

And lovely, still, the late gold light
And the mauve-breasted pigeons, plump with crumbs
And the blush of cassis in the wine
And the flicked cigarettes and the jangling coins
And the murmur of language we half-understand

And lovely how evening falls like silk
Along the river—*au revoir*
And how we've been loveliest, always, here
And how we've missed nothing, and how we'll be missed

III

Letter from Irena, in Warsaw, in Winter, Translated Loosely from the French

Dear Migratory Bird—

You wrote, "It is only when I travel when I manage to follow my soul."
This is so true, because it means this "âme" (the French prefer
to speak about "the spirit") not only is in movement
but is more in movement independent from our will.

The destination is less important than the pleasure one takes in
    moving through space.

Recently it is a sentence of Japanese, Matsuo Bashō, author of haiku,
who stopped (arrested) me. Here she is:
"Every day is a journey and the journey is itself a house."

My farm is 100 km from Warsaw, derisory distance,
but that saves me from the home-body life that would have killed my
    soul—
or, if you prefer, would have withered (branded) my spirit.

At home, nothing interesting. The winter beats its full
and the cockroach follows. Even Mishka, my bitch, has bad hair.

But spring is soon—the thought enchants me
and, at the same time, distresses me.
And this anguish is like a small delicious cake
for my winter sadness.

If you see Jorge, pass on to him my best regards.
And if I would write him a small word, to say
I did not know that he has such a beautiful moustache.

To us it snows but that gives a luminosity to the sky.
The crystal air has something of cleansing that lights the head.

But difficult to imagine that there were still some days
I walked barefoot by the sea.

Kisses and North Winds,
Irena

I had one white dress and I gave it away.
　　　　—Kathleen McGookey, from *Whatever Shines*

If What We Love Turns to Glass, How Do We Keep It Safe

I'd like to make something tender for both of us. Something, at least, to put into your hands. Something like those flowers I saw by the side of the road in the Polish countryside. Though some might call them weeds, as I might have called them once. But that summer evening, just after the storm, I walked along naming them to myself: *buttercup, thistle, poppy, homely oh lovely dandelion*. I thought them jewellike, there in the high grass; blue mist rising off the fields. Men on bicycles wobbling home. Everything softening in the blur of twilight: woodsmoke, drizzle, sky. I thought then, as I think now: so where's the line between beauty and sorrow; where's the line between terror and joy? How the small daughter of my friends had run out the open door of the house, screaming and laughing, into the rain. How your mother—still beautiful, still—had hobbled each day down the road to the store. How all those years you watched her disappear until she disappeared for good. How my father, those same years, adrift, drifted too far in his ship of bones; then only the smell of flowers above that bed where he'd lain to die. So I take your suffering, you take mine, we take it up—shall this be a bouquet? That evening in Poland I walked for an hour, away from then back toward the church. I called to no one, and no one called to me—though the warm room was waiting, the bread. I would give you this now: the pale green dome; the meadow; the quiet house, lights coming on. How the child, in her sleep, breathed the breath of birds. How the little boat of my heart goes out.

I'd Like a Love Letter and Too Much Light in My Eyes

I'd like a bird to fly into my left hand and sit there warming it, feather and pulse. I'd like to sleep with a big cat sometimes—mountain lion or tiger or lynx. But mostly I'd like to slide into a warm bath with you now. Steam in our eyes and our hair. So I've wanted too much. So where's the crime? Never flowers or jewels or a sleek limousine, though I've had those things. I would give them back. Or I would accept them again, every gift. So I've not settled down with some pots and pans, but loved the smooth sheets of each strange new bed. I can't seem to stay in one place long enough to ever get sick of it. Listen: you call to me, I'll come. I'll pack a bag full of lingerie and meet you, breathless, wherever you are. What can I bring you that you would lick from my fingers, like sugar, with your tender, feathery tongue? How else to spend ourselves but on love? You want the red lace against my breasts. You want nothing for breakfast. I want that, too.

Really, I Couldn't Say When My Kisses Got Closer to Your Mouth

—when that voice in my head that repeats, *You'll never be loved, you'll never be loved*, shut up. I tell you I loved, in the childhood story, how the tigers turned into butter and, in their turn, got eaten up. I keep thinking about the morning I woke and you were still sleeping, still holding my hand. Your face in that halo of fairy-tale curls. I keep thinking about a day I spent in the mountains, the sheep like clouds. Clouds with small, clumsy legs, but clouds. A farmer stood near his tasseled horse at the plow and smiled for the pictures I took. Red tassels. Loved creature. Loved. Now the house is locked up tight, and somewhere a siren keeps going off. Some wounds don't ever heal. But I like your woundedness, your mouth. I like thinking this will all come true, if we're brave and good enough. The girl won't be eaten by the witch. The boy will find the way back home through the woods by the small coins of bread on the path, by the moon. Really, I never know where it begins. The buttery longing turned to a sweetness too sweet to bear. Almost too sweet.

Because New Love Smells like Grass

Because messages fly between us—quick, quick—like the shadows of birds. Here, mist and blurred light, sheets of rain. There, your body pale as the snow that doesn't fall, almost luminous. Almost the sweet ghost of itself. And if I've loved before this weather all things sharpened, where's that edge? Would you describe your hands as calm? Your voice caught, nervous as a boy's. Well, I swore off swearing off the things that crave me long ago. When I was rushing for a train. When I was ridiculous with grief, my heart too heavy for its wheels. See, if you could see me now, you'd laugh, unbraid my hair. At least I hope that's what you'd do. Unwrap this black scarf from my throat. And then the rain would give us back the world within the world we made. When we leaned close, undid our names; you fed me chocolate from your palm. Now, snow. Now, sleep. Keep warm. This, too, will green again until there's no green left in it. God wants us not to turn our heads. My tongue a wing, if you believe in it, that makes you holy, slick.

You Simply Close Your Hand Around Whatever Shines

Dear Heart—I grow more and more fond of you. Fonder and fonder, like grass growing high and wild at the edge of a quiet pond. Of your hair, like tangled sun. Of your face, your eyes, your thoughtful hands. And whatever this is between us, we say, let's not give it any name. Which might stop its blossoming, we agree. Though it's not so much flowering as green. A green shoot to handle with tenderness now. As in: *to fondle*; as in: *to be fond*. We might skip stones on that pond's smooth surface, might gather weeds, but we'll keep our word. And jaded as we are, we can touch without irony. Kindly lie down. Your skin gives off some kind of light when you sleep, and I'm grateful for that. I would not want you hurt. We disappear from each other, come back, disappear. And those others we've called *beloved* part the curtain of high grass, a breeze.

The Silk of Longing Is Never Worth What We Are Paid

Oh lamb. Oh lonely in your rooms above the childless neighbors, too. The blue of afternoon went on and on like winter, didn't it? The first lights flickering at dusk along the street to make you sad. You took the subway into town, then taxied back, your meager store of cash diminishing again. And still awake at four A.M., you wanted anything but this: the silent bed; the empty kitchen; birdsong startling the trees. Open your hand and kiss your palm. That's my kiss, as real as salt. Then turn your head and kiss your shoulder, pale as snow, then, warm as milk. The day turns over when we sleep. We need our sleep. Take comfort there. I wish for you the book of childhood's secrets, love's dark stairs. I climbed them once to you; would climb again toward you now. And keep you company awhile. And lie down next to you. Oh lamb.

Then

On nights when there was no moon I carried water from the well.
I waded through hip-deep grass to hang my laundry on the line.

Then I hummed myself to sleep in a wooden room in a wooden house.
White moths fluttered over the bed and mornings, some mornings, a
   bird flew in.

I heard the creek running past at all hours, the barking of dogs, a
   tractor's distant thrum
through the bright haze of late afternoon. Some days I looked across a
   field

and the shadows were moving; the wildflowers bowed. Some evenings
I walked down the road in the rain in my flame-colored coat, not a
   stranger here,

and spoke, if I spoke at all, to a broken tree, and called that prayer.
Earth was a real place then and the house in the meadow was lit from
   within by a child.

Carpathia

Having rinsed off the soot and stink
of the Polish train,
having sung with the child.

Having eaten and laughed and wept,
had my vodka with apple juice,
my bread.

Having walked through the fields
at dusk, and into the forest
and back again—

meadows of buttercups,
thistles with bristling heads,
the first blue cornflowers of June.

Having opened my arms to the sky
falling back on itself
in my dizziness.

Having taken the small purple berries
that dropped from the wild bush
into my palm

—Siberian berries, like tiny plums—
put their sweet bitter inkiness
onto my tongue.

Having failed and failed at love.
Having gone anyway,
breath after breath.

Having trusted the world to be kind
and stood in the doorway
and listened for wolves

and heard my own dead in the high
grass whispering,
beloved, beloved, beloved.

Notes

"Postcard with Sarah, to Sarah, from a Bridge in Paris—Which?" is for Sarah Luczaj, as are "Postcard to Sarah, in the Carpathians, from Paris, the Rue Vieille du Temple" and "Postcard to Myself from the Lower Carpathians, Spring," which is also for Lukasz Luczaj.

"Shine" is for James Baker Hall and Mary Ann Taylor Hall.

"Greed" borrows its first line from Ann Fisher-Wirth's poem, "Liege, First Year, First Marriage," in her collection *Blue Window*.

"Postcard to Lisa, with Lisa, from Metro Line 1" is for Lisa Pasold.

"Mistake" is for my father, in memoriam, as are "Last Fever," "Watching Him Die," "Ghost Hunger," "Who Reminds Me of You, When You Could Still Walk—Just Barely" and "Seven Years After Your Death."

"Postcard Beginning with a Quote from Mark C., Avenue de l'Opéra" is for Mark Chapman.

"Postcard from Akhmatova's Bed" takes its first line from a poem by Ann Carson, "DIVORCE IN GENERAL IS A VERY DIFFICULT THING," from "T.V. Men: Akhmatova (Treatment for a Script)" in *Men in the Off Hours*.

"Postcard to X from Warsaw, Ulica Piękna ("Pretty Street")": for temporary residence on "Pretty Street," I thank my friend, Richard Boulez.

"Ground" is for my brother, John, and for my mother.

"Postcard to Ben, with Ben, from Paris, Kentucky" is for Ben Bealmear.

"Fireflies" is for my late aunt, Barbara Bakaysae.

"Postcard with Andrew, to Andrew, from I-75 on New Year's Day" is for Andrew Altamirano.

"Postcard to Carine from the Past" is for Carine Topal.

"Pantoum: le Jardin d'Isabelle" is for the Poilloux family. The first line is a variation on a line by H.D., "the love of my lover for his mistress," from her "Fragment Forty-one."

"Au Revoir, Paris," after the Greek poet Praxilla's "Loveliest of what I leave behind..." is for Elizabeth Iannaci.

"Letter from Irena, in Warsaw, in Winter, Translated Loosely from the French" is for Irena Wiszniewska.

Each of the prose poems in Section III takes its title from a poem in Kathleen McGookey's luminous collection, *Whatever Shines*.

ABOUT THE TITLE: "Carpathia" refers to the mountainous region in Eastern Europe from which my father's people came, a source of mystery throughout my childhood and a place that seemed to me, for a long time, more imaginary than real. A decade ago, I discovered that Carpathia is indeed an actual place—a wild and haunted and beautiful region, where borders have shifted and shifted again—and began to travel there. Its mysteriousness, for me, has not abated. Even the etymology of "Carpathia" is enigmatic: the name "Karpetes" may derive from the Archaic Polish word *karpa*, which meant "rugged irregularities, underwater obstacles/ rocks, rugged roots or trunks." Or the name may come from the Indo-European word *kwerp*, "to turn," akin to the Old English *hweorfan*, "to turn, change," perhaps referring to the way the Carpathian mountain range bends or veers in an L-shape. The name of the Carpi, a Dacian tribe, may have been derived from the name of the Carpathian Mountains. Alternatively, the mountain range's name may be derived from the name of the Dacian tribe. "Carpathia" was also the name of the ship that rescued the survivors from the Titanic. When the wreck of the *Carpathia* was discovered off the English coast in 1999—the same year, coincidentally, I first came to the Carpathians—the head of the rescue crew, Graham Jessop, noted, "She is in one piece, and she is upright." I'm grateful to my friend, Collin Kelly, for suggesting "Carpathia" as a title for this collection. It seems that all my journeys lead back to that place of grief and beauty and mystery and love.

Acknowledgments

Grateful acknowledgment is made to the editors of the following publications in which these poems or earlier versions of them previously appeared:

American Life in Poetry: "Anniversary";

Arsenic Lobster: "What Is This?";

Black Rock & Sage: "Postcard with Andrew, to Andrew, from I-75 on New Year's Day" (appeared as "New Year"), "Wish";

The Broadkill Review: "Seven Years After Your Death," "Whose Hunger," "Kind Weather," "Ghost Hunger" (published as "Food");

Connecticut River Review: "Lucifer, Full of Light," "Salt," "Who Reminds Me of You, When You Could Still Walk—Just Barely";

The Cortland Review: "Postcard to Ben, with Ben, from Paris, Kentucky" (appeared as "Bluegrass Rhapsody");

Java Monkey Speaks Anthology Vol. III: "My Old True Love";

Pool: "Postcard from Akhmatova's Bed" (appeared as "Akhmatova's Bed");

LimpWrist: "House," "Known," "Postcard to Lisa, with Lisa, from Metro Line 1";

Literary Imagination: "Greed" (appeared as "Midas");

Margie: "Watching Him Die";

New Delta Review: "Postcard to Sarah, with Sarah, from a Bridge in Paris—Which?," "Postcard to Ilya Kaminsky from a Dream at the Edge of the Sea";

New Letters: "Why I Believed, as a Child, That People Had Sex in Bathrooms";

The Other Voices International Project: "Anniversary," "Postcard to Myself from the Lower Carpathians, Spring," "Shine";

Polish American Studies: A Journal of Polish American History and Culture: "Postcard to Myself from the Lower Carpathians, Spring";

roger: "My Old True Love," "Postcard to Myself from the Lower Carpathians, Spring";

San Pedro River Review: "Mistake";

Tin House: "Lethe," "Postcard to X from Warsaw, Ulica Piękna ("Pretty Street")";

Upstairs at Duroc: "Be Always Late," "Postcard Beginning with a Quote from Mark C., Avenue de l'Opéra";

Verse Daily: "Anniversary";

When She Named Fire: An Anthology of Contemporary Poetry by American Women: "Why I Believed, as a Child, That People Had Sex in Bathrooms";

Wind: "Anniversary," "Shine," "Au Revoir, Paris," "Girl in a Truck, Kentucky Highway 245," "Ground."

A number of these poems also previously appeared in a chapbook, *Narcissus*, published by Tupelo Press, 2008.

"Fireflies" and "Carpathia" were chosen by Philip Levine to receive the 2009 *New Ohio Review* Prize in Poetry, and were published in the fall issue of the journal. The author is grateful to Mr. Levine and the editors of *New Ohio Review*.

About the Author

Cecilia Woloch was born in Pittsburgh, Pennsylvania, and grew up there and in rural Kentucky, one of seven children of a homemaker and an airplane mechanic. She attended Transylvania University in Lexington, Kentucky, earning degrees in English and Theater Arts, before moving to Los Angeles in 1979. She received her MFA in Creative Writing from Antioch University L.A. in 1999. A celebrated teacher, Woloch has conducted poetry workshops for thousands of children and young people throughout the United States and around the world, and since 2006 has been a lecturer in the creative writing program at the University of Southern California. She spends a part of each year traveling, and in recent years has divided her time between Los Angeles and Idyllwild, California; Atlanta, Georgia, and Shepherdsville, Kentucky; Paris, France, and a small village in the Carpathian Mountains of southeastern Poland.

BOA Editions, Ltd.
American Poets Continuum Series

Colophon

Carpathia, poems by Cecilia Woloch, is set in Monotype Dante. First created in metal type in the mid-1950s and digitalized in the 1990s, it is the result of a collaboration between Giovanni Mardersteig—a printer, book designer, and typeface artist renowned for the work he produced at Officina Bodoni and Stamperia Valdònega in Italy—and Charles Malin, one of the great punch-cutters of the twentieth century.

The publication of this book is made possible, in part, by the special support of the following individuals:

Anonymous
Alan & Nancy Cameros
Gwen & Gary Conners
Susan DeWitt Davie
Peter & Suzanne Durant
Pete & Bev French
Judy & Dane Gordon
Kip & Debby Hale
Tom & Illona Hansen
Bob & Willy Hursh
Peter & Robin Hursh
Nora A. Jones
Keith Kearney & Debby McLean
X. J. & Dorothy M. Kennedy
Laurie Kutchins
Jack & Gail Langerak
Rosemary & Lewis Lloyd
Boo Poulin
Deborah Ronnen & Sherm Levey
Steven O. Russell & Phyllis Rifkin-Russell
Vicki & Richard Schwartz
Pat & Mike Wilder
Glenn & Helen William

✴

Printed in the USA
CPSIA information can be obtained
at www.ICGtesting.com
JSHW082224140824
68134JS00015B/724